hummus

where the heart is

hummus

where the heart is

moreish recipes for
nutritious and tasty dips

Dunja Gulin

photography by Mowie Kay

RYLAND PETERS & SMALL
LONDON • NEW YORK

Senior Designer Sonya Nathoo
Commissioning Editor Alice Sambrook
Text Editor Kate Reeves-Brown
Head of Production Patricia Harrington
Art Director Leslie Harrington
Editorial Director Julia Charles
Publisher Cindy Richards

Food Stylist Emily Kydd
Prop Stylist Jo Harris
Indexer Vanessa Bird

First published in 2018 by
Ryland Peters & Small
20–21 Jockey's Fields, London WC1R 4BW
and 341 E 116th St, New York, NY 10029
www.rylandpeters.com

10 9 8 7 6 5 4 3 2 1

Printed in China

Text © Dunja Gulin 2018
Design and photographs ©
Ryland Peters & Small 2018

ISBN 978-1-84975-928-1

A CIP record for this book is available from
the British Library. US Library of Congress
cataloging-in-publication data has been
applied for.

Notes
• Both British (Metric) and American (Imperial
plus US cups) measurements are included in
these recipes for your convenience, however it is
important to work with one set of measurements
and not alternate between the two when
following a recipe.
• All spoon measurements are level unless
otherwise specified. A teaspoon is 5 ml and
a tablespoon is 15 ml.
• When a recipe calls for the grated zest of citrus
fruit, buy unwaxed fruit and wash well before
using. If you can only find treated fruit, scrub well
in warm soapy water before using.
• Everyone's hummus intake is different, but for
this book we have assumed an approximate
serving amount of 50 g/2 oz. hummus for one
small serving or 100 g/3½ oz. for one large
serving per person.

Contents

introduction

When you have been a vegetarian since you were fifteen years old, as I have, hummus inevitably becomes your staple food, your favourite snack and your go-to meal, regardless of where you are in the world. What also helps you to fall in love with this magic dish is coming from an Istrian family that has been cultivating chickpeas for decades, as I do.

Chickpeas are precious to us. The plant is prickly, and each bean comes in its own little pod that needs to be picked separately, one by one. When the pods have dried, we spread them over a big tarpaulin and my uncle drives over them with his tractor a couple of times to crush them. The chickpeas inside stay intact – their toughness always amazes me! Then we all lift the tarpaulin and start waving it so that the broken pods can fly away on the wind. It's not an easy job and we all appreciate this small bean so much more, knowing how demanding the whole process of cultivating it is.

Even today, more than twenty years after I decided to switch to a plant-based lifestyle, each time I visit my grandma I know that a 1-kg/2-lb. bag of dried chickpeas will be waiting for me on my way out. She always asks what I'll use them for, and I know if I tell her I'm making hummus and falafel she won't know what I'm talking about, so I often just tell her I'm making her yummy stew recipe or a salad, because that's what we usually use chickpeas for in my country. And it's not as if I'm lying, because I do enjoy them in many different recipes, but if I'm totally honest, I have to admit that they turn into hummus at least 70% of the time in my kitchen, because there's just nothing better than a bowl of dense and creamy hummus made from luke-warm chickpeas!

If you're used to store-bought hummus or the hummus served in restaurants, you won't know what the 'real thing' tastes like until you make it yourself from scratch. I hope this book will help you to re-discover this amazing dish! But why should we limit ourselves to the basic hummus recipe? There are so many wonderful and healthy ingredients that can be added to it, or that can be made into hummus-style dishes: other beans, lentils, vegetables, nuts, seeds, grains... When you add to that list all the things you can use hummus for: as a dip, spread, dressing, stuffing and even dessert, I can safely say that there can be a different type of hummus on your table every single day of the year! So let's roll up our sleeves together and get to cooking!

Dunja Gulin

cooking methods

The first thing you have to do to make a good hummus is cook
the chickpeas well, so that they are soft, easier to digest and can be
made into a creamy paste. I cook mine from scratch – it's a cheaper
and healthier option than using canned ones, and the resulting hummus
is divine. Dried chickpeas and beans need to be soaked for at least
12 hours before cooking. This step cannot be skipped as you could have
stomach-ache and bloating if they aren't soaked and cooked properly.

The most common methods for cooking
chickpeas and other hard beans (such as pinto,
haricot/navy, kidney, borlotti, black beans, etc.)
are pressure-cooking, boiling and the so-called
'shock method'.

Pressure-cooking

I prefer to use a good stove-top pressure cooker
for cooking beans, since it's easy, doesn't require
my constant attention and beans cooked this way
are softer and easier to digest. You do not need
to have an expensive type of pressure cooker
with a fancy lid that no one knows how to put
together; there are inexpensive, mechanical,
Italian-style models available, which will serve
you for decades! I have been using my pressure
cooker almost every single day for seventeen
years now, and it still looks brand new.

180 g/1 cup chickpeas or other hard beans
1.9 litres/8 cups water, for soaking
700 ml/3 cups water, or more if needed,
for cooking
2 dried bay leaves
5-cm/2-inch piece of kombu seaweed (optional)

Soak the chickpeas or other beans in the soaking
water for 12 hours. Drain, add to the pressure
cooker, cover with the fresh water for cooking
and bring to the boil. Drain, rinse well and cover
again with fresh water, 3–4 cm/1¼–1½ inches
above the level of chickpeas or beans. Add the
bay leaves and kombu (if using). Secure the lid
and allow to boil over a medium heat until it
starts hissing and the pressure valve comes up.
Reduce the heat to low (just enough to hear a
low hissing sound of the steam coming out of
the valve), and cook for 1 hour. Turn off the heat,
allow the pressure to drop and open the lid.

The chickpeas or beans should be soft. If not using
immediately, let cool, place in a glass container
with a tight lid covered in cooking water and keep
refrigerated. They can last for about 10 days.

Boiling

If you don't own a pressure cooker, you can cook chickpeas or other beans in a regular, heavy-bottomed pot by boiling them until soft. It usually takes longer than pressure-cooking, and the cooking time depends a lot on the type of beans used, their size and also how long they have been sitting on the shelf – beans that are older are harder and need to be cooked for longer.

180 g/1 cup chickpeas or other hard beans
1.9 litres/8 cups water, for soaking
820 ml/3½ cups water, or more if needed,
    for cooking
2 dried bay leaves
5-cm/2-inch piece of kombu seaweed
(optional)

Soak the chickpeas or other beans in the soaking water for 12 hours. Drain, cover with fresh water (enough to cover) and bring to the boil. Drain, rinse well and cover again with 820 ml/3½ cups of water for cooking. Add the bay leaves and kombu (if using). Let boil over a high heat, uncovered. With a slotted spoon, remove any foam that might appear. Lower the heat, cover and cook until tender; 1 hour or more. Check every 20 minutes and add more hot water if needed. The chickpeas or other beans should be tender when done.

Shock method

This method is a bit more demanding and requires your constant attention. You have to keep adding cold water during the cooking process, 'shocking' the hot beans to make their skins softer and easier to digest. The best type of pot to use is a heavy, cast-iron pot with a 'drop' lid that fits inside the pot. Beans cooked this way are sweeter-tasting and delicious.

180 g/1 cup chickpeas or other hard beans
1.9 litres/8 cups water, for soaking
600 ml/2½ cups water, plus more cold water for
    topping up, for cooking
2 dried bay leaves
5-cm/2-inch piece of kombu seaweed (optional)

Soak the chickpeas or other beans in the water for soaking for 12 hours. Drain, cover with fresh water (enough to cover) and let boil. Drain, rinse well and cover with the 600 ml/2½ cups of fresh water. Add the bay leaves and kombu (if using). Let boil over a medium heat, uncovered. With a slotted spoon, remove any foam that might appear. Lower the heat and float a lid that is smaller than the diameter of the saucepan on top of the beans. Keep an eye on the water level, removing the lid and adding more cold water down the side each time the water level becomes low. Continue cooking in this way until the chickpeas or beans are tender; 1–2 hours.

Chickpeas

basic hummus

This recipe will be the base for many recipes in this book! I encourage you to cook your own chickpeas according to the instructions on pages 8–9. Canned chickpeas can be used too (in this case, just use the cooking water from the can), but keep in mind that the deliciousness of the hummus made with freshly cooked, lukewarm chickpeas puts the bland-tasting versions made with canned chickpeas to shame!

320 g/2 cups cooked chickpeas (see page 8–9), plus 60 ml/¼ cup of the cooking liquid, or more if needed, plus 2 tablespoons cooked chickpeas to serve

2 tablespoons extra-virgin olive oil, plus 2 tablespoons to serve

1 tablespoon tahini

3 garlic cloves

freshly squeezed juice of ½ a lemon, or to taste

½ teaspoon salt, or to taste

freshly chopped flat-leaf parsley, to garnish (optional)

MAKES ABOUT 2–4 SERVINGS

Blend all the ingredients in a blender or food processor, except the extra chickpeas and olive oil to serve, slowly adding the cooking liquid until you reach a thick and creamy consistency; this will take about 1 minute. High-speed blenders make the creamiest texture and need less liquid and time, but both food processors and stick blenders can be used as well. Adjust the lemon juice and salt to taste.

Serve topped with 2 tablespoons extra-virgin olive oil and 2 tablespoons whole chickpeas. Garnish with chopped flat-leaf parsley, if you like.

sprouted chickpea hummus

Sprouting chickpeas is super simple and it transforms the hard seed that takes hours to cook into easier-to-digest quick-cooking sprouts! Blanching them also improves the taste and texture.

135 g/¾ cup dried chickpeas

1.25 litres/5 cups water

3 tablespoons tahini

2 teaspoons ground cumin

¼ teaspoon smoked paprika, plus extra to garnish

2 garlic cloves

1 tablespoon olive oil

freshly squeezed juice of ½ a lemon, or to taste

½ teaspoon salt, or to taste

rice cakes and pickled vegetables (such as radishes, cucumber and red onion), to serve (optional)

MAKES ABOUT 2–3 SERVINGS

Soak the dried chickpeas in water overnight. The next day, drain well, place in a big jar, cover with muslin/cheesecloth and secure with a rubber band. Place in a bowl at a 45° angle, top-down, so that any extra water can easily drain off. Let sprout for 24 hours.

Run cold water through the muslin/cheesecloth to cover the chickpeas, then drain well and place back in a jar. Repeat this for another 24 hours. By now a tiny sprout should already show on top of each seed. I like to sprout for another 24 hours (3 days in total), so each seed has a tail at least half the size of the chickpea itself. Some beans sprout more slowly than others, so adjust your sprouting time. You can store sprouted chickpeas, well drained and air-dried, in a clean jar in the fridge for a couple of days. You should have 300 g/3 cups of sprouts.

For the hummus, bring the water to the boil, add the sprouted chickpeas and cook over a medium heat for 10 minutes. Drain well (saving at least 60 ml/¼ cup of cooking liquid), and let cool slightly.

Blend with all the other ingredients, adding just enough cooking liquid to make a creamy hummus. Adjust the seasoning to taste. Sprinkle with smoked paprika and drizzle with olive oil just before serving. Serve warm or cold. I love spreading it on puffed rice cakes, topped with slices of lightly pickled vegetables – simple yet delicious!

spinach hummus

There are never enough greens in our diet! It's especially important not to over-cook the green leafy vegetables, but they can also be used raw, the way I'm using spinach in the following recipe. This way, all the nutrients remain intact and the hummus becomes vibrantly green!

320 g/2 cup cooked chickpeas (see page 8–9), plus 60 ml/¼ cup of the cooking liquid, or more if needed

3 tablespoons extra-virgin olive oil

1 tablespoon cashew butter

3 garlic cloves

1 tablespoon umeboshi vinegar (not essential, but adds gusto)

70 g/1 handful raw spinach leaves

freshly squeezed juice of ½ lemon, or to taste

½ teaspoon salt, or to taste

freshly chopped flat-leaf parsley, to garnish (optional)

Vegetable Crisps/Chips (see page 87), to serve (optional)

MAKES ABOUT 2–3 SERVINGS

Blend all the ingredients in a blender or food processor, slowly adding the cooking liquid until you reach a thick and creamy consistency; this will take about 1 minute. (High-speed blenders make the creamiest texture and need less liquid and time, but both food processors and stick blenders can be used as well.)

Adjust the lemon juice and salt to taste. Garnish with chopped flat-leaf parsley, if you like, and serve with vegetable crisps/chips for dipping.

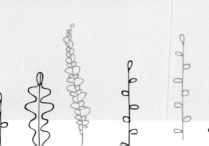

Greek-style hummus

I grew up on a Mediterranean diet, but the Greeks give it a slightly different spin; I had a chance to spend half a year in Greece in my late teens and was snacking on Kalamata olives probably for a good part of my days there!

320 g/2 cups cooked chickpeas (see page 8–9), plus 60 ml/ ¼ cup of the cooking liquid, or more if needed

2 tablespoons extra-virgin olive oil, plus extra to serve

1 tablespoon tomato purée/paste

1 teaspoon Greek floral honey (or other)

2 garlic cloves

freshly squeezed juice of ½ a lemon, or to taste

1 tablespoon salted capers, well washed and drained, plus extra to serve

25 g/¼ cup stoned/ pitted Kalamata olives, chopped, plus extra to serve

1 tablespoon fresh oregano leaves or 1 teaspoon dried oregano, plus extra to serve

salt, if needed (capers and olives are salty)

MAKES ABOUT 2–4 SERVINGS

Blend the chickpeas, olive oil, tomato purée/paste, honey, garlic and lemon juice in a food processor or blender until smooth; about 1 minute, slowly adding the cooking liquid to reach the desired consistency.

Stir in the capers, olives and oregano. Taste and adjust seasoning.

Top with extra capers, chopped black olives, oregano and a drizzle of olive oil to serve, if you like.

fried mushroom hummus

My goal in this recipe is to show you that sautéed mushrooms need not be mushy and chewy. If prepared properly, they soak up the spices but stay compact and crunchy, and can be added to leftover hummus. You can 'posh up' this dish by serving it in baked mushroom caps!

250 g/9 oz. mushrooms (shiitake, cremini, button or portobello)

3 tablespoons dark sesame oil

2 tablespoons tamari soy sauce

1 teaspoon agave or maple syrup (optional)

1 teaspoon freshly squeezed lemon juice

1 quantity Basic Hummus (see page 12)

freshly ground black pepper

portobello mushrooms, baked, to serve (optional)

micro herbs or cress, to garnish (optional)

MAKES ABOUT 3-5 SERVINGS

Wipe the mushrooms with a wet cloth to remove any dirt. If using shiitake, remove the stems. Roughly chop the mushrooms. Heat the oil in a wok or large frying pan/skillet, add the chopped mushrooms and stir well.

Add the tamari and syrup (if using), stirring until the mushrooms absorb the tamari, but remove from the heat before they start sweating. Add the lemon juice and some black pepper to taste. Stir into the freshly made hummus.

Serve in baked portobello mushroom caps, garnished with micro herbs or cress if you like.

hummus with hazelnut butter

Using different nut butters instead of the traditional tahini is a very interesting way to give classic hummus a makeover! You can substitute hazelnut with almond or walnut butter in this recipe too.

FOR THE HAZELNUT BUTTER
300 g/2 cups hazelnuts

FOR THE HUMMUS
320 g/2 cups cooked chickpeas (see page 8–9), plus 60 ml/ ¼ cup of the cooking liquid, or more if needed

2 tablespoons hazelnut butter (see above)

1 tablespoon good-quality balsamic vinegar

½ teaspoon fennel seeds, crushed

¼ teaspoon allspice, plus extra to garnish

grated zest and freshly squeezed juice of 1 lemon, plus extra grated zest to garnish

½ teaspoon salt, or to taste

2 tablespoons roasted hazelnuts (reserved from the hazelnut butter), roughly chopped

MAKES ABOUT 2–3 SERVINGS

Preheat the oven to 180°C (360°F) Gas 4.

For the hazelnut butter, place the hazelnuts on a baking sheet in one layer. Roast in the preheated oven for 12 minutes, stirring once. Take out one hazelnut – if the skin is peeling off easily and the inside is getting golden brown, they are ready. If not, roast for another 3–4 minutes. Take out of the oven, transfer to a bowl and let cool for 15 minutes. Set aside 2–3 tablespoons of whole hazelnuts to garnish.

In a high-speed blender, blend the rest of the warm hazelnuts using the blender's tamper to push down the hazelnuts. Start with a low speed and be patient. Depending on the quality of your blender, this might be quick or it might take a little longer. After a while, hazelnut flour will start turning into a smooth, oily butter. Transfer to a jar and use sparingly, both in sweet and savoury recipes. Cover when completely cool. Because of the high oil content, the butter will keep for months at room temperature. But it's so delicious I doubt it will last that long!

For the hummus, blend all the ingredients until smooth; about 1 minute. Taste and adjust the seasoning. Garnish with reserved chopped hazelnuts, grated lemon zest and a sprinkle of allspice. Rye crackers or crispy apple slices are great hazelnut-hummus dippers!

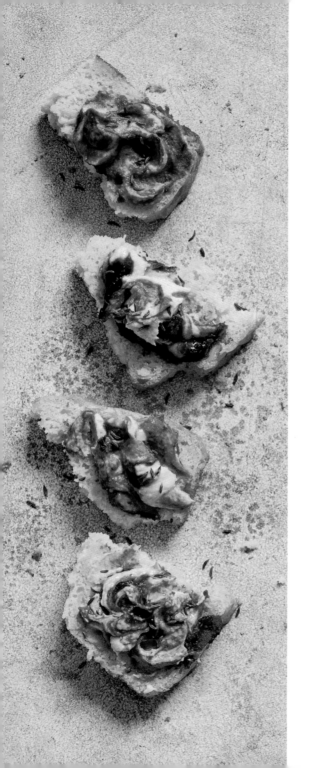

purple beetroot/ beet hummus

The earthy intense sweetness of baked beets adds a deep, rich flavour to this hummus.

2 beetroots/beets, well washed, with skin

1 quantity Basic Hummus (see page 12)

1 teaspoon caraway seeds

salt

olive oil, for drizzling

baking sheet lined with baking parchment

MAKES ABOUT 2–4 SERVINGS

Preheat the oven to 200°C (400°F) Gas 6.

Rub a pinch of salt into the beetroots/beets. Wrap them well in aluminium foil. Place on the lined baking sheet and bake in the preheated oven for about 45 minutes, or until the beetroot/beet flesh is soft. Let cool slightly. Peel, discard the skins and tops and blend in a blender or food processor into a smooth purée.

Blend the beetroot/beet purée into the basic hummus a little at a time (reserving a little to swirl in at the end if, you like). It should be done slowly until the desired consistency, colour and taste is reached. Taste and adjust the seasoning. Stir through the caraway seeds or sprinkle on top. Swirl through any reserved beetroot/beet purée and drizzle with extra olive oil to serve, if you like.

curry-spiced hummus

Here's a hummus for all of you curry-lovers out there! Serve it with homemade chapatis (see page 72) for a complete Bhārata experience!

2 tablespoons coconut oil

1 large onion, finely chopped

1 tablespoon fresh ginger, very finely chopped

2 garlic cloves, very finely chopped

1 tablespoon mild curry powder

2 teaspoons ground ginger

2 teaspoons ground turmeric

2 teaspoons garam masala

2 teaspoons ground coriander

1 teaspoon yellow mustard seeds

¼ teaspoon ground cinnamon, or to taste

¼ teaspoon chilli/chili powder, plus extra to garnish

¼ teaspoon kala namak (or rock salt)

1 tablespoon tomato purée/paste

2 tablespoons soy sauce

60 ml/¼ cup coconut milk, or more if needed

320 g/2 cups cooked chickpeas (see page 8–9)

salt

freshly chopped coriander/cilantro, to garnish (optional)

MAKES ABOUT 2–3 SERVINGS

Melt the coconut oil in a frying pan/skillet. Add the finely chopped onion, ginger and garlic along with a pinch of salt, and sauté, stirring constantly, until fragrant.

Add all the spices, kala namak or rock salt, tomato purée/paste and soy sauce, and continue stirring until the ingredients start sticking to the pan and browning. Add a couple of tablespoons of the coconut milk to deglaze the pan.

Blend together with the chickpeas into a creamy hummus, adding the remaining coconut milk until the desired consistency is reached.

Garnish with extra chilli/chili powder and freshly chopped coriander/cilantro, if you like. Enjoy!

onion jam hummus

Sautéing onions for a longer period of time can sound a bit daunting, I know. That's why making a bigger batch of this jam in one go is very practical since it keeps well stored in jars and can be used up during the year as a delicious condiment or added to dishes like hummus!

80 ml/⅓ cup olive oil

1 kg/2 lb. 4 oz. onions, cut in thin half-moons

50 g/¼ cup muscovado sugar

80 ml/⅓ cup good-quality wine vinegar

60 ml/¼ cup white wine

a splash of soy sauce

1 quantity Basic Hummus (see page 12)

salt and freshly ground black pepper

seeded, wholegrain or raw crackers, to serve

MAKES ABOUT 4–8 SERVINGS

For the onion jam, add the oil to a heavy-bottomed pan, heat slightly, then add onions and a pinch of salt. Stir over a very low flame, uncovered, until the onion liquid thickens (this takes about 2 hours).

Mix the sugar, wine vinegar, white wine, soy sauce, salt and plenty of freshly ground black pepper into the onions, and boil down into a paste (can be thicker or runnier, as preferred). This makes enough for 5 x 210-ml/7-fl. oz. jars of onion jam. Keep in the fridge for about 2 months, or it can be pasteurized in the oven and will then keep for a year at room temperature.

To make the hummus, mix in about 240 ml/1 cup (or one of your jars, if easier) of the onion jam into the basic hummus.

I often load the hummus with extra onion jam to serve and eat as a bruschetta topping or with seeded, wholegrain or raw crackers.

caramelized carrot hummus

Carrots are a sweet root vegetable, and you can emphasize that sweetness even more by long, slow sautéing in oil. Rosemary gives such a nice Mediterranean touch to the whole combination, making this hummus one of my favourites!

4 carrots

5 tablespoons light sesame oil or olive oil, plus a little extra to serve

¼ teaspoon coarse sea salt

2 sprigs of rosemary or 2 teaspoons dried rosemary needles

1 tablespoon soy sauce

1 tablespoon dark agave nectar

1 quantity Basic Hummus (see page 12, but omit the olive oil since we're adding oil to the carrots)

MAKES ABOUT 3–5 SERVINGS

Wash and scrub the carrots, then cut into large bite-size pieces (Chinese 'rolling-style' cutting technique is the best choice for this dish). Heat the oil in a cast-iron wok or stainless-steel heavy-bottomed pan, over medium heat. Add the carrots and sprinkle with the coarse sea salt. Stir well, coating all the carrot pieces in oil. Once they start sizzling, lower the heat, add the rosemary sprigs/needles and sauté for at least 20 minutes, or longer, stirring constantly to avoid burning the carrots. Do not cover – you want the carrots slow-fried.

The carrots are ready when they shrink to half of their original size, and become very soft and fragrant. At the end of sautéing, add the soy sauce and agave, and stir quickly over high heat until absorbed.

Two options to serve: you can either blend the carrots into the hummus, or, as I prefer to do, just stir the caramelized carrots into the hummus and serve. This way, once you start eating you'll occasionally bite into a fragrant piece of carrot – the taste just explodes in your mouth!

Other root vegetables such as parsnip, parsley root, celeriac/celery root and even sweet potato can be caramelized this way. Try adding other spices of choice, too!

Mediterranean tomato hummus

This hummus is packed full of Mediterranean flavours. I usually bake garlic bulbs once a week, then squeeze out the flesh and keep it in an airtight container in the fridge to use in different recipes.

1 garlic bulb

10 sun-dried tomato halves

320 g/2 cups cooked chickpeas (see page 8–9), plus 60 ml/ ¼ cup of the cooking liquid, or more if needed

1 tablespoon tahini

3 tablespoons extra-virgin olive oil (2 for the hummus and 1 to serve)

1 bunch of fresh basil, chopped, plus a few whole leaves to garnish

1 sprig of thyme, leaves only

3 tablespoons chopped parsley leaves

2 teaspoons lemon juice

½ teaspoon salt, or to taste

¼ teaspoon dried rosemary powder

freshly ground black pepper

coarse sea salt and 1 teaspoon olive oil, for baking the garlic

MAKES ABOUT 2–3 SERVINGS

Preheat the oven to 180°C (360°F) Gas 4.

Brush the garlic head with oil, rub in some coarse sea salt, wrap in aluminium foil and bake for 40 minutes or until the garlic flesh becomes soft. Use half of the amount in this recipe and save the remaining paste to add to other dishes.

Soak the sun-dried tomato halves in warm water for 30 minutes. Drain and discard the soaking water. (If using oil-packed tomato halves, there's no need to soak them, but omit 2 tablespoons of olive oil in the recipe, since the tomatoes will bring enough oil to the hummus.) Chop finely.

Blend the chickpeas with the tahini, slowly adding the cooking liquid, until it has reached the desired consistency. Spoon it out into a bigger bowl and stir in the chopped tomato halves, half the garlic bulb paste, chopped basil, the thyme leaves, 2 tablespoons of the olive oil, 2 tablespoons of the chopped parsley, the lemon juice, salt and freshly ground black pepper to taste. Sprinkle with the dried rosemary powder and the remaining chopped parsley, and garnish with the whole basil leaves and a drizzle of olive oil. Use as a bruschetta topping or as a dip for sesame grissini.

spicy baked chickpea hummus

Rolling the cooked beans in a spicy marinade and baking or frying them before blending into a creamy dip makes a really special hummus!

FOR THE BAKED CHICKPEAS

2 tablespoons soy sauce

½ teaspoon chilli/chili powder

½ teaspoon ground turmeric

½ teaspoon ground ginger

½ teaspoon smoked paprika

2 tablespoons sesame or olive oil

320 g/2 cups cooked chickpeas (see page 8–9), washed and well drained, plus 60 ml/¼ cup of the cooking liquid, or more if needed

FOR THE HUMMUS

2 garlic cloves

1 tablespoon tahini

¼ teaspoon salt, or to taste

freshly squeezed juice of 1 lime

dried chilli/hot red pepper flakes, to serve

1 tablespoon toasted sesame oil or olive oil, to serve

MAKES ABOUT 2–3 SERVINGS

Preheat the oven to 200°C (400°F) Gas 6. Choose the 'upper and lower heating element with fan' setting.

For the baked chickpeas, in a medium bowl, whisk together the soy sauce, chilli/chili powder, ground turmeric, ground ginger, smoked paprika and sesame or olive oil. Add the cooked chickpeas (set aside the reserved cooking liquid for later) and mix well so that all the chickpeas are coated. Place in one layer on a baking sheet lined with parchment paper. Bake in the preheated oven for 10 minutes, stirring every 3 minutes, or until the chickpeas start drying out and browning. (Alternatively, the marinated chickpeas can also be pan-fried, until browned and fragrant.)

Reserve 2 tablespoons of the baked chickpeas to serve, and place the rest into a blender or food-processor. Blend with the remaining hummus ingredients, and slowly add the reserved chickpea cooking liquid until it reaches a thick and creamy consistency; 1-2 minutes. High-speed blenders make the creamiest texture and need less liquid and time, but both food processors and stick blenders can be used as well.

Adjust the lime juice and salt to taste. Serve with the reserved whole baked chickpeas, a sprinkle of chilli/hot red pepper flakes and a drizzle of oil on top.

Beans and lentils

Caribbean-style hummus

I visit a couple of different Caribbean islands each year while cooking on a vegan cruise, and I love tasting local food in each port. Using pineapple and mango in savoury dishes was a novelty for me the first time I tasted their specialities, but not anymore! Try this spicy and fruity hummus, each mouthful will take you straight to the tropical sunny beach – you'll feel like you're on holiday.

160 g/1 cup fresh pineapple chunks

2 tablespoons virgin coconut oil

320 g/2 cups cooked kidney beans (see page 8–9), plus 60 ml/ ¼ cup of the cooking liquid

1 tablespoon almond or cashew butter

1 teaspoon fine garlic powder

grated zest and freshly squeezed juice of 1 lime

½ teaspoon salt, or to taste

2 tablespoons mango hot sauce

finely sliced spring onions/scallions, to garnish (optional)

Chapatis (see page 72) and lime wedges, to serve

MAKES ABOUT 2–4 SERVINGS

In a heavy-bottomed pan or wok, over a high heat, fry the pineapple pieces in coconut oil until slightly browned, stirring constantly.

Add the remaining ingredients and mash them together into a chunky hummus, adding enough of the cooking liquid to incorporate. Blending would make a brownish coloured mush and the dip wouldn't look so appetizing, so leaving chunks of pineapple and bean makes it bright-coloured and interesting.

Sprinkle with sliced spring onions/scallions, if you like, and serve with chapatis and lime wedges for squeezing.

haricot/navy bean hummus

On special occasions, or when I want to win over a healthy-food sceptic, this is my dip of choice. The price of pine nuts can be discouraging, but here we're using a really tiny amount with a lot of impact on the final taste, since pine nuts carry a pine tree aroma that no other nut offers.

50 g/⅓ cup pine nuts

320 g/2 cups cooked haricot/navy beans, well drained

1 garlic clove

2 tablespoons plant-based cream (soy, oat, etc.)

½ teaspoon salt, or to taste

¼ teaspoon ground rosemary

a handful of fresh basil, chopped, plus a few leaves to garnish

10 slices wholemeal/ whole-wheat baguette or ciabatta, freshly toasted

2 tablespoons olive oil

peppercorn mix, freshly ground, to taste

MAKES ABOUT
2–5 SERVINGS

In a heavy-bottomed frying pan/skillet dry-roast the pine nuts until fragrant and golden, stirring constantly. Be careful as they can turn brown in a matter of seconds! Set aside 2 tablespoons of whole roasted pine nuts, to serve.

Blend the remaining roasted pine nuts in a blender or food processor with the haricot/navy beans, garlic, cream, salt and rosemary into a creamy hummus. Stir in the chopped fresh basil.

Toast the baguette slices just before serving, then top with haricot/navy bean hummus. Decorate each slice with whole pine nuts, basil leaves, a drizzle of olive oil and top with freshly ground peppercorn mix.

tofu and rice hummus

I'm a big fan of properly cooked short grain brown rice and always having some left-over cooked rice in the fridge helps me create a healthy meal in no time. It's so easy to blend these simple ingredients into a creamy hummus-like dip, and it can be used in variety of ways: as a healthy snack with raw veggie sticks or crackers, as a topping for pizza, or as a sandwich spread.

150 g/⅔ cup short-grain brown rice, cooked

200 g/1⅓ cup fresh soft tofu

60 g/½ cup finely chopped onion

1 tablespoon white tahini

1 tablespoon umeboshi vinegar or 2 teaspoons umeboshi paste

1 tablespoon nutritional yeast (optional)

½ teaspoon salt, or to taste

TO SERVE

2 tablespoons olive oil

seeded toast

shredded red cabbage

diced avocado

pea shoots

freshly ground black pepper

MAKES ABOUT
2–3 SERVINGS

Blend the cooked rice, tofu, onion, tahini, umeboshi vinegar or paste and about 3 tablespoons of water for 1–2 minutes or until smooth. Depending on how soft your tofu is, you might need to add more water, little by little, to achieve a consistency of thick cream cheese.

Serve on seeded toast, topped with shredded red cabbage, diced avocado and pea shoots (or other vegetables of your choice), with a drizzle of olive oil and some freshly ground black pepper.

Note: This hummus tastes better if left to rest in the fridge for 24 hours. Try dark sesame oil instead of olive oil, for a slightly different aroma.

black bean hummus

Black beans are very nutritious and should be used regularly as part of a healthy weekly family menu. They are particularly creamy and tasty if soaked and cooked at home, so if you are using canned beans in this recipe, expect a less creamy texture. Also, more spices and flavourings will need to be added to compensate for their bland taste.

FOR THE SALSA VERDE
25 g/1 cup roughly chopped flat-leaf parsley

60 ml/¼ cup olive oil

2 tablespoons capers, rinsed and drained

½ tablespoon apple cider vinegar

1 tablespoon freshly squeezed lemon juice

2 garlic cloves, crushed

½ teaspoon salt

FOR THE HUMMUS
320 g/2 cups cooked black beans

70 g/1 small onion, finely chopped

¼ teaspoon chilli/chili powder, or to taste

freshly squeezed juice of ½ a lemon

½ teaspoon salt, or to taste

freshly chopped flat-leaf parsley, to garnish

MAKES ABOUT
2–3 SERVINGS

For the salsa verde, blend all the ingredients for 1–2 minutes to obtain a green oily paste.

For the hummus, roughly mash the cooked beans with a fork, add the remaining ingredients along with the salsa verde, and stir with a wooden spoon until everything is well incorporated. Taste and adjust the seasoning.

Garnish with freshly chopped parsley. Serve with tortilla chips or other crunchy dipper of your choice.

spicy red lentil hummus

Once properly cooked, red lentils turn into a creamy thick purée all by themselves, so there is no need to blend.

130g/⅔ cup red lentils, washed and well drained

480 ml/2 cups hot water

4 cm/1½ inches kombu seaweed (optional)

1 bay leaf

1 tablespoon smoked paprika, plus extra to garnish

¼ teaspoon cayenne pepper, or to taste

½ teaspoon salt

2 garlic cloves, crushed

1 tablespoon Dijon mustard

freshly squeezed lemon juice, to taste

2 tablespoons olive oil

1 tablespoon umeboshi vinegar (optional, for umami taste)

2 tablespoons freshly chopped flat-leaf parsley

MAKES ABOUT
2–3 SERVINGS

Place the well-drained lentils into a heavy-bottomed saucepan, add the hot water, kombu (if using) and bay leaf. Bring to the boil over a medium flame, lower the heat, half-cover and let simmer for 10 minutes. Stir and cook until all the lentils fall apart, forming a soft purée (do not add any extra water unless absolutely necessary – usually this 1:3 lentil to water ratio is just right). At the end of cooking, add the smoked paprika, cayenne pepper and salt to taste.

Remove from the heat, add the garlic, mustard, lemon juice, olive oil and umeboshi vinegar (if using). Mix well and let sit for at least 1 hour before serving – the purée will thicken and develop a nicer flavour. If you're in a hurry, spread the hot purée on a baking sheet and let it cool for 20 minutes. It should thicken and, when well mixed, have a hummus consistency.

Sprinkle with a little smoked paprika and freshly chopped flat-leaf parsley to garnish. Serve with red chicory/endive leaves, broccoli and/or asparagus spears, or any other steamed or raw vegetables of your choice.

Eastern European-style hummus

Borlotti beans, sweet and smoked paprika, fried onions and pepper: all of these ingredients are Eastern European favourites used in many different dishes – so why not combine them into a hummus-like dip too?

3 tablespoons sunflower oil

1 onion, finely chopped

1 carrot, finely chopped

1 small sweet red romano/babura pepper, finely chopped

3 garlic cloves

1 teaspoon each smoked paprika and sweet paprika

1 tablespoon tomato purée/paste

½ vegetable stock/ bouillon cube

320 g/2 cups cooked borlotti or pinto beans (see page 8–9), plus a litle reserved cooking liquid

salt and freshly ground black pepper

toasted bread, to serve

mixed vegetable pickles, to serve (such as cauliflower, pepper, carrots, onions)

freshly chopped flat-leaf parsley, to garnish

MAKES ABOUT
2–3 SERVINGS

Heat the oil in a pan and sauté the vegetables with a pinch of salt until soft and fragrant. Add the spices, tomato purée/paste, stock/bouillon cube and ground black pepper to taste, and stir well. Sauté for another minute.

Roughly mash the cooked beans. Add to the pan, mix well to incorporate the sautéed vegetables, adding a little cooking liquid to get a chunky paste. Taste and adjust the seasoning.

Serve on toasted bread, topped with mixed vegetable pickles and a sprinkle of chopped flat-leaf parsley.

Veggies and nuts

courgette/zucchini hummus

Courgettes/zucchini are one of those veggies that, once they are in season, just won't stop growing! Throughout July we have so many of them in our garden that I have to keep inventing new recipes to use them up. They are delicious just grilled/broiled as described in the recipe, but blending them into a creamy hummus-like dip intensifies their sweet flavour.

800 g/2 large courgettes/ zucchini (or several smaller ones)

2 tablespoons olive oil

½ teaspoon coarse sea salt

finely grated lemon zest, to garnish

baking sheet lined with baking parchment

MAKES ABOUT
1–2 SERVINGS

Preheat the oven to its maximum temperature (usually 250°C (475°F) Gas 9) and choose the 'grill with fan' setting. Slice the courgettes/zucchini into 5 mm/¼ inch thick slices (if using 2 large ones, slice them into rounds crossways; if using smaller ones, slice them lengthways).

In a small bowl, mix together the oil and salt. Neatly arrange them in a single layer on the lined baking sheet and brush with the oil and salt.

Bake for 15–18 minutes or until the courgette/zucchini slices start browning. Reserve a few slices to serve and transfer the remaining slices to a food processor or blender and blend for 1–2 minutes, or until smooth and creamy. Serve topped with the reserved courgette/zucchini slices and garnish with lemon zest.

Note: If you feel the hummus is too simple-tasting, you can add the classic hummus ingredients – 2 garlic cloves, freshly squeezed juice of ½ a lemon and 1 tablespoon tahini.

sweet potato and coconut hummus

Amazing sweet potatoes make an even more amazing hummus-like dip, especially when combined with velvety coconut milk and a touch of spices. So healthy and so good!

4 orange sweet potatoes

¼ teaspoon coarse sea salt

130 g/⅔ cup cooked chickpeas (see page 8–9), well drained

½ teaspoon ground ginger

2 garlic cloves

grated zest and freshly squeezed juice of 1 lemon

¼ teaspoon cayenne pepper

1 tablespoon coconut aminos or soy sauce, to taste

60 ml/¼ cup full-fat coconut milk, or more if needed

shaved coconut, unsweetened, to serve

olive oil, for drizzling

mixed micro herbs, to garnish

baking sheet lined with baking parchment

SERVES 2–4

Preheat the oven to 200°C (400°F) Gas 6.

Scrub, dry and prick the sweet potatoes. Rub in the salt.

Place the whole sweet potatoes on the lined baking sheet and bake for 50 minutes or until the flesh is completely soft. Let cool slightly, cut in half and spoon out the flesh into a bowl. Save the skins to serve.

Blend the sweet potato and chickpeas in a food processor or blender with garlic, lemon zest and juice, cayenne pepper and aminos for about 1 minute, until smooth, adding coconut milk to reach the desired consistency.

Spoon into the reserved potato skins and sprinkle with shaved coconut. Drizzle with olive oil and scatter with mixed micro herbs to garnish.

fermented foods hummus

As a fermented-foods enthusiast, I'm always trying to incorporate home-fermented foods into our meals. Anything that has undergone the process of wild fermentation has an intense umami taste and is more nutritious and much easier to digest. Make your own rejuvelac and kimchi following recipes from my cookbook on fermented foods, or buy good-quality kimchi in a health-food shop. Just look for unpasteurized fermented products, if available.

320 g/2 cups cooked chickpeas (see page 8–9)

2 tablespoons toasted sesame seeds or 1 tablespoon tahini

1 tablespoon olive oil

2 garlic cloves, minced

60 ml/¼ cup rejuvelac or brine from fermented vegetables/ kimchi, or more if needed

2 tablespoons white miso paste

100 g/1 cup spicy kimchi, chopped, plus extra to garnish

¼ teaspoon salt, or less if using salty brine

Japanese micro herbs such as micro mizuna, to garnish (optional)

MAKES ABOUT
2–4 SERVINGS

Blend the chickpeas with sesame seeds/tahini, olive oil, garlic, rejuvelac or brine and miso paste in a food processor or blender for 1 minute, adding just enough liquid to get a smooth paste.

Stir in the chopped kimchi, taste and add salt, if needed. Scatter with extra chopped kimchi and micro herbs to garnish, if you like.

triple pumpkin hummus

Vegetable-based hummus-like dips are much lighter and easier to digest than their bean-based counterparts, and they're also a great option when we need fresh ideas on how to use up seasonal veggies! Starchy vegetables like pumpkin, squash and sweet potato are the best choice – they are creamy and rich and make a delicious faux-hummus!

700 g/4 thick slices dense pumpkin (Hokkaido or Kabocha are my favourites)

½ teaspoon coarse sea salt, or to taste

3 tablespoons pumpkin seed oil

4 tablespoons shelled pumpkin seeds (green)

2 garlic cloves

2 tablespoons umeboshi vinegar (for umami taste)

a splash of lemon juice (optional)

hot water, as needed

freshly ground black pepper, to serve

baking sheet lined with baking parchment

MAKES ABOUT
2–4 SERVINGS

Preheat the oven to 180°C (360°F) Gas 4.

Peel the pumpkin slices and cut them into tablespoon-size pieces. Sprinkle with a little coarse sea salt and 1 teaspoon of the oil. Bake in the preheated oven until very soft; about 40 minutes.

Wash the pumpkin seeds and drain well. Dry-roast over medium heat in a frying pan/skillet, stirring constantly to avoid burning. The seeds are ready once they puff up and start cracking. Set aside 1 tablespoon for the garnish.

Blend the baked pumpkin pieces in a blender or food processor until smooth, adding 2 tablespoons of the pumpkin seed oil, the garlic, umeboshi vinegar (or more salt), lemon juice (if using) and just enough hot water to get a creamy faux-hummus. Stir in the roasted pumpkin seeds for a little crunch.

Serve drizzled with the remaining pumpkin seed oil, a sprinkle of roasted seeds and a good grinding of black pepper, if you like. This is delicious eaten with seeded crackers such as the ones on page 75.

cashew and avocado hummus

A light, summery dip! I love its creamy texture and the bright pastel green colour – it is great served on toasted sourdough bread or with pitta breads (see page 80), for dipping.

70 g/½ cup cashews, plus extra, chopped, to garnish

130 g/½ ripe avocado, stoned/pitted and peeled

30 g/¼ cup chopped onion

freshly squeezed juice of ½ a lemon

2 tablespoons toasted sesame seeds or 1 tablespoon tahini

scant ½ teaspoon salt, plus a pinch for soaking the cashews

freshly ground black pepper, to serve

garlic chives, to garnish (optional)

MAKES ABOUT 2 SERVINGS

Cover the cashews in water, add a pinch of salt and soak for a couple of hours or overnight.

Rinse and drain the cashews well. Place all the ingredients in a blender or food processor and blend for 1 minute to obtain a smooth creamy paste.

Serve immediately, with a good grinding of black pepper, on toasted sourdough bread or with pitta breads. Garnish with extra chopped cashews and garlic chives, if you like.

Any leftovers should be kept covered and refrigerated – the outer layer of this dip browns, so stir well once again just before serving.

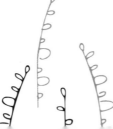

pea and basil hummus

This thick hummus-like spread made with green peas is so good! The texture always surprises me, since peas might seem light and watery, however, the finished dip has an amazing smooth texture, strong flavour and punchy colour. A simple recipe, but delicious and very lunch-worthy!

720 ml/3 cups water

260 g/2 cups fresh or frozen peas

10 g/½ cup basil, plus a few leaves to garnish

1 tablespoon olive oil, plus extra for drizzling

2 garlic cloves

2 tablespoons sunflower seed butter

½ teaspoon cumin seeds, dry-roasted and crushed (optional)

½ teaspoon salt, or to taste

MAKES ABOUT 2–4 SERVINGS

Bring the water to the boil, add the peas and cook, covered, until soft but still green (about 8–10 minutes). Drain, saving the cooking water. Blend in a food processor or blender with all the other ingredients until thick and creamy, adding about 60 ml/¼ cup of the cooking liquid as necessary. Drizzle with extra olive oil to serve, if you like.

cauliflower hummus

This is a lighter version of hummus, both colour- and taste-wise, but delicious nonetheless! It makes a delicious, creamy soup, if more water is added at the end of blending or to the leftovers from the day before.

400 g/1 head of cauliflower, leaves removed

120 ml/½ cup hot water, or more if needed

2 tablespoons olive oil, plus extra for drizzling

2 tablespoons tahini

2 garlic cloves

1 teaspoon ground cumin, plus extra toasted, to garnish

1 teaspoon ground coriander

1 tablespoon umeboshi vinegar (optional)

freshly squeezed juice of ½ a lemon, or to taste

salt and freshly ground black pepper

finely grated lemon zest, to garnish

MAKES ABOUT
2 SERVINGS

Cut the cauliflower into big florets, place in a heavy-bottomed pan, add the hot water and a pinch of salt, and cook, covered, over a medium heat until the cauliflower is soft but not mushy. Drain and save the cooking liquid.

Blend the cooked cauliflower with the oil, tahini, garlic, spices and umeboshi vinegar (if using) in a blender or food processor. Add the lemon juice, some salt and pepper and blend again, adding the cooking water (and more water if needed), to reach the desired thickness. Taste and adjust the seasoning. Let sit for at least 30 minutes before serving. However, it tastes even better served the next day!

Drizzle with olive oil, then sprinkle with ground toasted cumin seeds and some finely grated lemon zest, just before serving.

walnut and red pepper hummus

This is the ideal choice for all who wish to enjoy the velvety texture of hummus with an extra kick of nutrients provided by raw and totally fresh ingredients! This hummus can be made well in advance – it will taste even better if it sits in the fridge for a couple of days.

300 g/2 cups walnuts, shelled

80 g/⅔ cup diced onion

½ bunch parsley

2 tablespoons olive oil

1 tablespoon tahini

1 teaspoon salt

¼ teaspoon chilli/chili powder

2 garlic cloves

1 tablespoon sweet paprika

1 red (bell) pepper, seeded

umeboshi vinegar, to taste (or substitute with lemon juice and a little soy sauce)

garlic chives and mixed micro cress or herbs, to garnish

MAKES ABOUT 2–3 SERVINGS

Cover the walnuts with plenty of water and let soak for a couple of hours or overnight with a pinch of salt. Rinse and drain. Blend all the ingredients in a high-speed blender for 1 minute into a velvety hummus. For weaker blenders, you might need to add a little water during blending.

This recipe is so versatile, it can be used as a dip for raw veggies, a sauce for spiralized courgettes/zucchini, or even as a filling for raw sushi. Here, it is spread on mini toasts and garnished with mixed micro cress and herbs as a canapé.

baked aubergine/eggplant hummus

The texture of baked aubergine/eggplant just begs to be made
into a delicious hummus-like dip, so here it is. Onions, dates, spices and
vinegar all contribute to its rounded taste, so don't skip these ingredients!

**860 g/2 large
aubergines/eggplants**

50 ml/¼ cup olive oil

¾ teaspoon sea salt

**120 g/1 cup sliced
onions**

**½ teaspoon fennel
seeds**

**½ teaspoon cumin
seeds**

**¼ teaspoon chilli/chili
powder**

**30 g/¼ cup soft
dates, soaked**

**2 tablespoons tamari
soy sauce**

**80 g/½ cup cooked
chickpeas, blended
into a paste**

**2 tablespoons apple
cider vinegar**

**freshly chopped mint
leaves, to garnish
(optional)**

**baking sheet lined with
baking parchment**

MAKES ABOUT
4–6 SERVINGS

Preheat the oven to 200°C (400°F) Gas 6.

Wash the aubergines/eggplants and cut them
lengthways in half. Oil the cut sides with some
of the oil and rub with a little of the salt. Prick the
outer skin of all four halves with a fork. Lay them
on the lined baking sheet, cut-side down. Bake in
the preheated oven for 40 minutes or until soft to
the touch. Let cool a little before peeling off the
skin. Chop the flesh into small dice.

While the aubergines/eggplants are baking,
sauté the onions with the remaining salt in the
remaining olive oil over a low heat, stirring
occasionally. Add the fennel and cumin seeds and
chilli/chili powder, cover and continue sautéing
until completely soft and caramelized, but not
browned. This will take about 20 minutes.

Add the drained and chopped dates and
aubergine/eggplant flesh and sauté for 5 minutes
more. Now add the blended chickpeas, tamari
and vinegar, stir well, and cook uncovered for
another 5 minutes. Serve garnished with chopped
mint, if you like. This hummus can keep in the
fridge for about a week.

Dippers

chapatis

This is a great hummus-dipper, especially for Indian-spiced hummus. In case you're avoiding yeasty breads, chapatis are a great alternative, and so easy to make!

150 g/1 cup wholemeal/ whole-wheat flour, plus extra for dusting

150 g/1 cup unbleached plain/all-purpose flour, plus extra for dusting

½ teaspoon sea salt

140 ml/generous ½ cup lukewarm water

2 tablespoons sesame or olive oil

MAKES 10 CHAPATIS, 13 CM/5 INCHES IN DIAMETER

Put both flours in a bowl. Add the salt and oil, and whisk to combine. Gradually add the water and knead to form a smooth, medium-soft dough. Kneading is crucial, so do not skip this step and continue kneading until you get the right consistency (depending on the flours you're using, you might need to add a bit more flour or water). Wrap in clingfilm/plastic wrap and set aside for 15 minutes to rest.

Divide the dough into 10 equal portions and form each portion into a ball, rolling them until smooth and without cracks. Coat each ball in flour and roll out them out into chapatis, 13 cm/5 inches in diameter, with the help of a rolling pin. Lightly coat each chapati in flour on both sides to prevent from sticking.

Heat a cast-iron or stainless-steel pan over a medium heat and start frying. The chapati is ready for turning when bumps appear on its surface, but it shouldn't brown. Turn it onto the other side and flip again once the bumps appear. After the second flip, leave it in the pan for a moment, and then gently press the chapati around its edges with a kitchen towel or oven mitt. It should puff up in the middle! Continue with the remaining chapatis. Serve immediately or cover with a kitchen towel to prevent drying out.

red pepper and buckwheat crackers

The ingredients for these crackers might sound a bit weird, since I'm not adding any flour, and raw veggies go directly into the dough, but please give this recipe a chance and you'll discover how healthy ingredients can also make delicious crackers! Great choice as a hummus dipper if health-conscious foodies are coming over for a snack.

270 g/1½ cups buckwheat, soaked in water overnight and well drained

5 tablespoons flax or chia seeds, soaked in water, plus 1–2 tablespoons extra for sprinkling

½ teaspoon sea salt

100 g/1 medium red (bell) pepper

60 g/½ cup chopped onion

1 tablespoon sweet paprika

¼ teaspoon smoked sweet paprika, plus extra for sprinkling

110 ml/½ cup pure carrot juice or water

MAKES 12-16 CRACKERS

In a high-speed blender blend all the ingredients into a thick paste. Use a tamper to push down the mix to get a smooth texture.

Cut a piece of baking parchment to the size of your oven rack/ baking pan and place it on a smooth surface (kitchen counter or table). Spoon the cracker paste onto the baking parchment and spread to get a rectangle-shaped even surface. If you like really crunchy crackers, the dough should be almost paper-thin, but if you like a bit of texture, roll to desired thickness. Sprinkle the dough evenly with extra soaked flax or chia seeds and a couple of pinches of smoked sweet paprika. Put the oven rack/baking pan on the edge of the counter and quickly pull the baking parchment with the cracker paste to slide onto it.

Place in the top of the oven; turn on the fan and the heat up to 100°C (200°F). Prop the door open with a folded kitchen towel, to ensure proper dehydration. Dehydrate for 2–3 hours.

Check the cracker dough and, if it isn't sticky, peel off the baking parchment and break into your desired shapes. Further dehydrate the crackers directly on the oven rack until dried. If you have a dehydrator, use it – you know what you have to do! Store in a ziplock bag in the fridge.

sesame grissini

Grissini are delicious on their own, but pairing them with hummus for a snack or a nutritious appetizer is a great idea, especially if sesame seeds are added into the grissini dough! That way, even if there was no tahini in the house for the hummus, you still get a kick of sesame!

140 ml /⅔ cup lukewarm water

5 g/scant 2 teaspoons active dry yeast

5 g /1 teaspoon barley malt (or agave syrup)

190 g /1½ cup unbleached plain/all-purpose flour

60 g/½ cup wholemeal/ whole-wheat flour

4 g/scant 1 teaspoon salt

2 tablespoons raw, unhulled sesame seeds, plus 1 tablespoon extra for sprinkling

3 tablespoons light sesame or olive oil

2 baking sheets lined with baking parchment

MAKES 20 GRISSINI (APPROX. 35 CM/ 14 INCHES LONG)

In a small bowl, combine the water with the yeast and malt. Whisk and let sit for 15 minutes. The yeast will start to foam lightly.

In a separate bowl, combine the flours, salt, sesame seeds and 2 tablespoons of the oil. Stir in the bubbly yeast mixture and knead until smooth; about 4 minutes. Place on a lined baking sheet. With the help of a silicone spatula, oil the dough lightly. Let rise in the oven with only the light on, for 1 hour.

Preheat the oven to 180°C (360°F) Gas 4.

Form the dough into an oval shape and, with the help of a sharp wide knife, cut 1-cm/⅜-inch strips of dough. Stretch each strip with your fingers into a long grissino; some strips will be longer and thicker, so you'll be able to stretch two or three grissini out of them. From this amount of dough, you should get 20 grissini (35 cm/ 14 inches long and 1 cm/⅜ inch thick). They do puff a little while baking. I never use a rolling pin to stretch them since that flattens them and pushes out the air, which results in tough grissini.

Place the stretched grissini on the second lined baking sheet, 7 mm/¼ inch apart. Brush with the remaining oil and sprinkle with the extra sesame seeds. Bake in the preheated oven for 12–15 minutes in two batches, rotating them halfway through. Let cool and, if any are left, store in a sealable bag. Serve with any leftover hummus you might have in the fridge, or with freshly made hummus, still warm.

caraway seed focaccia bread

This dough takes a bit of time, but it's so worth the wait! No one can resist the delicious smell of freshly baked focaccia.

FOR THE STARTER
40 g/¼ cup rye flour

55 ml/¼ cup lukewarm water

9 g/1 tablespoon active dry yeast

FOR THE DOUGH
200 g/1½ cups unbleached spelt flour, plus extra for kneading

30 g/¼ cup wholemeal/ whole-wheat flour

4 g/scant 1 teaspoon salt

110 ml/½ cup lukewarm water

1 tablespoon olive oil, plus extra for drizzling

1 tablespoon soy milk

2–3 teaspoons of caraway seeds (or fennel seeds or dried oregano)

1 teaspoon coarse sea salt

23 x 30-cm/9 x 12-inch baking pan, well oiled

MAKES 1 LOAF

Mix together the starter ingredients, cover and let sit for 30 minutes.

Mix the flours and salt in one bowl and mix the water, olive oil and soy milk in another bowl. Add the liquids to the starter, incorporate well and then gradually add the flour mixture. Mix the dough with a wooden spoon, and then knead on a floured surface for 5 minutes, or longer, until soft and slightly sticky. Add flour as you knead, but not more than necessary. Place in a big oiled bowl, and oil the surface of the dough, too. Cover with a wet cloth and let rise for 2½ hours in a warm place.

Once risen, shape the dough to fit the oiled baking pan by gently pressing down from the centre towards the edges. Make dimples by poking the dough with your fingertips. Drizzle with olive oil, cover and let rise again for 2 hours. Do not skip this step, as the end result will be much tougher without this second rising.

Preheat the oven to 180°C (360°F) Gas 4.

Sprinkle the dough with the dried caraway seeds and coarse salt. Bake in the preheated oven for 20 minutes, or until golden and crisp. Let cool slightly before cutting.

Focaccia sandwiches are exceptionally popular with my family and friends – I cut 1 focaccia into 6 equal pieces, cut them in half lengthwise, spread hummus on the bottom half, top that with smoked tofu or baked tempeh, and add as many vegetables, pickles, sprouts and greens as I can fit inside. It's a complete meal in itself, very nutritious and very filling!

pitta bread

Making good pitta breads at home is just a matter of following a well-tested recipe – and having enough patience to knead the dough for 10 minutes!

FOR THE STARTER

80 ml/⅓ cup lukewarm water

2 teaspoons maple sugar or another sweetener

9 g/1 tablespoon active dry yeast

FOR THE DOUGH

400 g/3¼ cup plain/ all-purpose flour, plus extra for dusting

100 g/¾ cup wholemeal/ whole-wheat flour

1½ teaspoons sea salt

2 tablespoons olive oil, plus extra for oiling

270 ml/1 cup plus 2 tablespoons lukewarm water

dough scraper (optional)

baking sheet lined with baking parchment

MAKES 10 PITTAS

Whisk together the starter ingredients and rest, covered with a damp towel, in the oven with the light on for 30 minutes or until slightly bubbly.

In a large bowl, whisk together the flours and salt for the dough. Add the water and oil, and mix in with a wooden spoon. Knead the dough, first inside the bowl, then on a clean surface for 10 minutes. Don't add extra flour – the dough should be sticky but will come together eventually. Using a dough scraper helps initially.

Oil both the bowl and the dough, place the dough in the bowl, cover with a damp towel and let rise in the oven, with the oven light on, for 3 hours or until doubled in size. It's even better if you can make the dough a day ahead and let it rise in the fridge overnight.

Preheat the oven to its maximum (usually 250°C (475°F) Gas 9) and choose the 'lower heat element with fan' setting if you can. Weigh out about 10 small 80-g/3-oz. portions) of dough, place on a floured surface and let rise for another 10 minutes.

On a floured surface, gently roll each ball into a 15-cm/6-inch circle. Use a spatula to flip them over as you put them on the lined baking sheet, so the floured side is on top. Four should fit on one sheet.

Open the preheated oven and slide the baking paper with the pittas directly onto the bottom of the oven, without the tray. Bake for 5 minutes until puffed up and lightly browned on the bottom. Open the oven, slide the baking paper with done pittas back onto the baking sheet and repeat with the remaining dough. Wrap in a clean kitchen towel until ready to serve. Freeze any leftovers.

cornbread

Baking powder-leavened breads have a more cake-like consistency, but where I come from, we make and serve our cornbread as a bread; mildly salty, with soups and stews or spread with delicious hummus!

500 ml/2 cups kefir whey (or use 375 ml/1½ cups soy milk or soy yogurt plus 125 ml/½ cup sparkling water)

1 tablespoon apple cider vinegar

2 tablespoons olive oil

200 g/1½ cup fine yellow cornmeal/polenta

170 g/1¼ cup plain/all-purpose or spelt flour

40 g/¼ cup chickpea flour (gram flour)

2 teaspoons baking powder

1½ teaspoons bicarbonate of soda/baking soda

1 teaspoon salt

1 tablespoon coarse cornmeal/polenta, for sprinkling

30 x 12-cm/12 x 4¾-inch bread pan, oiled

MAKES 1 LOAF

Preheat the oven to 220°C (425°F) Gas 7.

In a large bowl, whisk all the wet ingredients. Sift in all the dry ingredients, except the coarse polenta for sprinkling, then combine them to get a smooth batter, but do not over-mix.

Pour the batter into the oiled bread pan, even the top with a spatula and sprinkle the coarse polenta over the whole surface – this will give the cornbread a nice top crust.

Bake for 25 minutes on the bottom of the oven, then move into the middle and bake for another 8 minutes or until the bread starts to turn golden and the corners begin to separate from the pan. The baking time and position in the oven highly depends of the type of oven, so make sure to adjust it to your conditions.

Let it cool in the pan for 5 minutes, then turn it out of the pan onto a wire rack and let cool for 30 minutes before cutting. Keep wrapped in a kitchen towel.

Note: whey and soy milk/yogurt are rich in protein and work best combined with cornmeal. Do not substitute with other plant-based milks, as they would make this bread very crumbly and difficult to slice.

rye crackers with chia seeds

You can either dip these crackers into hummus after they've cooled down, or you can spread any hummus you have over them, then top that with raw or fermented veggies and munch your worries away!

130 g/¾ cup rye flour

130 g/¾ cup unbleached plain/all-purpose flour

15 g/2 tablespoons chia seeds

4 g/scant 1 teaspoon salt

freshly ground black pepper, to taste

60 ml/¼ cup olive oil or light sesame oil

60 ml/¼ cup water

1 teaspoon dark agave or maple syrup

hummus, cucumber and micro cress, to serve (optional)

baking sheet lined with baking parchment

MAKES 12-16 CRACKERS

Combine all the dry ingredients in a large bowl. Emulsify all the wet ingredients with a whisk, and then slowly add them to the flour and seed mixture, stirring until well combined. The dough should quickly form a ball and shouldn't be sticky. Knead a couple of times; just enough to make sure all the ingredients are evenly distributed. Wrap in clingfilm/plastic wrap and let sit at room temperature for 10 minutes. Resting the dough makes rolling it out much easier.

Preheat the oven to 200°C (400°F) Gas 6.

Divide the dough into three equal pieces. Roll out a very thin layer of dough between two sheets of baking parchment. If you like really crunchy crackers, the dough should be almost paper-thin, but if you like a bit of texture, roll to desired thickness.

Use a knife or pizza cutter to cut out shapes. Squares or rectangles are practical choices, since you'll have not much leftover dough. Transfer the crackers to the lined baking sheet using a thin spatula or a knife. Prick each a couple of times with a fork.

Bake for 4–7 minutes, depending on the thickness of the crackers. Remember, they shouldn't brown, just get slightly golden. They will firm up as they cool, so don't expect them to be cracker-crunchy straight out of the oven.

Here, they are spread with hummus and topped with cucumber and micro cress, but you can eat them how you prefer! Store in an air-tight container after they've cooled completely.

vegetable crisps/chips

Who doesn't like using regular potato crisps/chips as a hummus dipper? However, the heavy feeling you get after eating fried foods (and other side effects such as weight-gain, skin problems, etc. that are experienced if this becomes a regular habit), might be a good reason to consider switching to no-fry veggie crisps/chips, which are highly nutritious, burst with flavour and the only side effect of eating them is health and happiness!

400 g/3 large carrots

400 g/2 large beetroots/ beets (you can use regular or a mix of golden or candied)

400 g/3 large parsnips

3 tablespoons olive oil

1 teaspoon fine sea salt

MAKES ABOUT
4–6 SERVINGS

Scrub all the root vegetables well and remove the tops and any black spots. Using a mandoline, slice them lengthways to get the longest strips possible. Small pieces will shrink into bite-size crisps/chips. Also, the slices should not be see-through thin.

Place in separate bowls and add 1 tablespoon of oil and ⅓ teaspoon salt to each batch. Mix thoroughly.

Place on dehydrator trays in a single layer and dehydrate for 2 hours on maximum temperature, then lower the temperature to 50°C/100°F and dehydrate for another 5 hours, or until crispy.

Do not expect them to be as crunchy as deep-fried crisps, but their amazingly rich taste will compensate for that, and I'm sure they'll become one of your favourite hummus dippers!

homemade corn tortilla chips

I prefer making tortilla chips without adding any other type of flour except for the finely ground yellow cornmeal, because I love the taste and the texture, and it also means they are gluten-free! However, these tortilla chips have to be eaten soon after baking, since they turn pretty hard and chewy after they cool down completely. Substitute half of the amount of cornmeal with wheat or spelt flour if you want them to keep well for longer.

150 g/1 cup finely ground yellow cornmeal

½ teaspoon sea salt, or to taste

1 tablespoon sesame seeds

1 tablespoon olive oil

240 ml/1 cup boiling water

MAKES 20–24 TRIANGLE-SHAPED CHIPS

Preheat the oven to 150°C (300°F) Gas 2.

In a bowl, combine the finely ground yellow cornmeal, salt and sesame seeds. Whisk, then add the oil and boiling water. Stir until well incorporated; you should get a soft dough, but not sticky.

Cut two pieces of baking parchment to the size of your baking sheet. Place one paper on the work surface and top with the dough, then top the dough with the second paper. Use a rolling pin to roll out the dough about 1 mm/1⁄16 inch thick.

Bake in the preheated oven for 10 minutes. Take out and mark with a knife into triangle shapes, or shapes of your choice. Continue baking for another 7–10 minutes, just until the dough stops being soft. Overbaking will make the chips too hard, so be careful! Let cool and break into the marked shapes. Serve the same day with one of the hummus recipes!

love your
leftovers

chunky hummus burgers

My favourite veggies to use in this recipe are grated beetroots/beets – they make these burgers bright pink, which makes them, in turn, very popular with kids! They have often been called 'Hello Kitty' burgers by my small guests!

200 g/1 cup leftover chickpea-based hummus

80 g/½ cup couscous

125 ml/½ cup boiling water

50 g/¼ cup finely grated vegetables (beetroots/beets, carrots, parsnip, celeriac/celery root, etc.)

40 g/1 small onion, finely chopped

2 garlic cloves, finely chopped

½ teaspoon dried oregano

2 tablespoons finely chopped parsley or finely snipped chives

salt and freshly ground black pepper, to taste

burger buns, vegan mayonnaise, lettuce, sliced gherkins and red onions, to serve (optional)

baking sheet lined with baking parchment

MAKES 6 BURGERS

Preheat the oven to 180°C (360°F) Gas 4.

Place the couscous in a bowl, pour over the boiling water, cover and let sit for 5 minutes.

Place all the ingredients in a mixing bowl and knead into a well-combined dough. Divide the mixture into 6 portions and form them into even burgers with your hands. Place them on the lined baking sheet.

Bake in the preheated oven for 20–25 minutes, or until a nice crust forms and the burgers start browning lightly. Here, these are served in a bun with vegan mayonnaise, lettuce, gherkins and red onion. But the trimmings are really up to you!

vegan devilled 'eggs'

We have plenty of baby potatoes in our garden in July, and each year I'm trying to come up with new recipes for how to use them. Vegan devilled eggs are so tasty and a great way to use up leftover hummus! The skin on the potatoes should just be scrubbed instead of peeled, if possible. It adds a wonderful earthy aroma. Yummy!

480–600 g/6 egg-sized baby potatoes

1 tablespoon olive oil

160 g/1 cup leftover hummus

¼ teaspoon ground turmeric

½ teaspoon sweet or spicy smoked paprika, to serve

micro coriander/cilantro, to garnish (optional)

salt

baking sheet lined with baking parchment

MAKES 12 'EGGS'

Preheat the oven to 200°C (400°F) Gas 6.

Scrub the potatoes well if using baby potatoes with delicate thin skins; otherwise peel them. Cut them in half lengthways and rub in the oil and a little salt. Bake in the preheated oven, cut-sides up, for 40–45 minutes or until golden and soft.

Meanwhile, warm up the hummus, add the turmeric and mix well to incorporate.

When the potatoes are done, let them cool slightly, then spoon some of the potato flesh out of each half and add 1½ tablespoons of hummus to each.

Sprinkle with smoked paprika and micro coriander/cilantro to garnish, if you like. Enjoy!

Olivier salad with hummus

Olivier Salad is a popular dish in many European countries. It's usually drowning in mayonnaise. One time I didn't have enough tofu mayo for a vegan version, so I used some hummus instead and it worked so well!

250 g/2 potatoes

150 g/1 cup peas, fresh or frozen

180 g/3 small carrots, diced

4–5 whole cucumber pickles, diced

½ apple, cored and diced

60 g/1 small onion, diced

4 tablespoons finely chopped parsley leaves or snipped chives, plus extra to garnish

200 g/1 cup leftover chickpea-based hummus

150 g/1 cup fresh tofu

4 tablespoons olive oil, plus extra to taste

½ teaspoon of salt, or to taste

2 tablespoons apple cider vinegar, plus extra to taste

freshly ground black pepper

SERVES 2–3

Boil the potatoes in their skins until soft but not overcooked. Let cool, then peel and dice. Set aside.

In a medium pan, bring 750 ml/3 cups water to the boil. Add the peas and cook until soft but still bright green. To save time, place a steamer basket or a fitting colander on top of the pot while the peas are cooking and steam the diced carrots, covered, until soft. In a bigger bowl, combine the peas, carrots, potatoes, diced pickles, apple, onion and parsley/chives.

Place the leftover hummus and fresh tofu in a blender or food processor. Blend them and, while blending, add enough water to obtain a creamy mayonnaise-like consistency that can be easily poured over vegetables, but isn't too watery! Add the olive oil, salt and apple cider vinegar – the hummus mayo should taste a little strong to complement the bland-tasting veggies.

Pour over the prepared veggies and mix well to coat. Taste and add pepper and more salt, vinegar or oil, as needed. Garnish with extra chopped parsley leaves or snipped chives. This salad tastes even better the next day!

millet and hummus porridge

When mornings start becoming cold and foggy in late autumn/fall and especially during winter, I often crave something more substantial for breakfast. Stirring some leftover hummus into freshly cooked porridge adds extra nutrients, creaminess and taste to your morning meal, and will keep you warm and satisfied until lunchtime!

100 g/½ cup hulled millet

480 ml/2 cups water

100–200g/½–1 cup leftover chickpea-based or bean-based hummus

salt

1 tablespoon toasted nuts or seeds, to serve

pickles or fermented vegetables, to serve

SERVES 2–3

Wash and drain the millet. Place it in a bowl and add the water. Soak overnight.

Cook the millet over a low heat, half-covered, for 20 minutes, whisking occasionally and adding more hot water if necessary, until it reaches a soft porridgey consistency. Add a pinch of salt at the end of cooking.

Remove from the heat and stir in the hummus until well incorporated. Serve sprinkled with the toasted nuts or seeds, along with pickles or fermented veggies, if you like – the crunch of the nuts/seeds and the fresh sour taste of the veggies complement the creaminess of the porridge.

If you're in a hurry, you can substitute millet with rolled oats, which do not need soaking before cooking.

deep-fried hummus bites

In the mood for some comfort food? I've got creamy, deep-fried hummus coming your way! It's quite rich, but sometimes you just want something a tad golden, crispy and oily on your plate.

200 g/1 cup leftover chickpea-based or bean-based hummus, at room temperature (the consistency should be quite thick)

240 ml/1 cup sunflower oil, for frying

lemon slices, micro herbs, tamari and ginger sauce and/or grated mooli/daikon or radish, to serve

FOR THE TEMPURA BATTER

70 g/½ cup plain/all-purpose flour, chilled

110 ml/½ cup ice-cold water

¼ teaspoon ground turmeric

salt, to taste

MAKES 6–8 BITES

To make the batter, with a whisk, quickly mix the chilled flour with the cold water, and add the turmeric and salt. Do not over-mix; some lumps are ok. To make the tempura crispy, it's very important to use cold ingredients, not mix too much and use the batter for frying immediately.

Heat the oil in a frying pan/skillet.

Using a tablespoon, gently slide spoonfuls of the hummus into the tempura batter and catch it with the same spoon when entirely coated. Drain any extra batter and gently lower the hummus into the hot oil. Fry until slightly golden. It's best to fry one spoonful at a time, to avoid burning.

Drain on paper towels and serve immediately with fresh lemon slices, micro herbs and a small bowl of tamari and ginger sauce. Grated mooli/daikon or radish is also a nice addition – they help in the digestion process of any fried foods.

hummus mezze

A mezze is a classic Middle Eastern or Eastern Mediterranean way to enjoy hummus, as part of a feast with lots of other small dishes that can be shared. Just add my tabbouleh, falafel and similarly themed trimmings of your choice.

FOR THE BROWN RICE TABBOULEH

340 g/2 cups diced tomatoes

¼ teaspoon salt

2 tablespoons salt-cured capers

320 g/2 cups cooked short-grain brown rice

40 g/1 cup finely chopped flat-leaf parsley

20 g/½ cup finely chopped basil or mint

1½ tablespoon olive oil

2 tablespoons finely chopped onion

2 tablespoons toasted sesame seeds

1 tablespoon apple cider vinegar

freshly ground black pepper

SERVES 4

FOR THE PUMPKIN-SEED FALAFEL

240 g/2 cups pumpkin seeds

6 sun-dried tomato halves, soaked

20 g/½ cup finely chopped fresh basil

20 g/½ cup finely chopped flat parsley

½ teaspoon dried oregano

2 garlic cloves, crushed

1 tablespoon olive oil

1 tablespoon lemon juice, or to taste

¼ teaspoon salt, or to taste

MAKES 12 BALLS

BROWN RICE TABBOULEH

Place the diced tomatoes in a colander, add the salt, mix to combine well and let sit for 15 minutes. Drain all the extra juice away. Wash, drain and chop the capers.

Stir all the ingredients together well. Let sit for 1 hour or overnight before serving.

PUMPKIN-SEED FALAFEL

Grind the pumpkin seeds into fine flour in a small electric spice grinder or blender. Drain and chop the sun-dried tomatoes very finely. Add the chopped tomatoes to the seed flour together with all the remaining ingredients, and mix well with your hands or with a silicone spatula. Wrap in clingfilm/plastic wrap and let sit in the fridge for 30 minutes. Pull off portions of the mixture (about the size of small walnuts) and roll into balls.

stuffed courgettes/zucchini

Another of my summer go-to courgette/zucchini recipes. Barley is often my grain of choice during the summer months, but feel free to use up any leftover cooked grains you might have in the fridge.

500 g/1 large courgette/zucchini

1 tablespoon olive oil

60 g/1 medium onion, chopped

¼ teaspoon ground turmeric

½ teaspoon oregano

1 tablespoon tomato purée/paste (optional)

1 tablespoon tamari soy sauce

130 g/¾ cup cooked barley (or other grains)

2 tablespoons chopped parsley leaves

100 g/½ cup leftover hummus

salt

purple basil or mixed salad leaves, drizzled with lemon juice, to serve

baking sheet lined with baking parchment

SERVES 2 AS A MAIN COURSE, 4 AS AN APPETIZER

Preheat the oven to 180°C (360°F) Gas 4.

Wash and cut the courgette/zucchini into three equal pieces crossways. Cut each piece in half lengthways. With a sharp spoon or knife, scoop out the seeds, making space for the filling. Save the scooped flesh to use for a soup or stew. Brush each courgette/zucchini piece with the olive oil and season with a pinch of salt.

In a heavy-bottomed pan over a medium heat, dry-fry the chopped onion with a pinch of salt, stirring often. Add the turmeric, oregano, tomato purée/paste and tamari, and stir until fragrant and browned. Add the cooked barley, parsley and hummus, and stir well until incorporated.

Place the courgette/zucchini pieces on the prepared baking sheet and divide the stuffing amongst them. Bake in the preheated oven for 20 minutes or until the courgette/zucchini flesh gets slightly soft. Serve with purple basil or mixed salad leaves drizzled with lemon juice.

hummus pizza

Vegan pizza with hummus? Hell, yeah! The pitta dough makes a perfect pizza crust, with a few slight adjustments. You make the whole amount of dough, use half for this pizza and the other half the next day to make pittas! The dough will keep wrapped in the fridge for two days.

½ quantity Pitta Bread dough (see page 80)

FOR THE TOPPING
300 g/1½ cups Basic Hummus (see page 12)

90 g/1 onion, cut into half-moons

8 green olives, stoned/pitted

2 garlic cloves, thinly sliced

80 g/1 cup button mushrooms, very thinly sliced

1 teaspoon dried oregano or pizza seasoning

2 handfuls rocket/arugula, to serve

8 cherry tomatoes, cut in half, to serve

2 tablespoons olive oil, to serve

MAKES 2 X 24-CM/9½-INCH DIAMETER PIZZAS

Follow the instructions for making the dough on page 80 to the rising stage. Preheat the oven to its maximum temperature (usually 250°C (475°F) Gas 9) and choose the 'lower heat element' setting.

After the rising of the dough, divide it into two balls (each should weight around 200 g/7 oz.) and place them on a floured surface. Let rise for another 10 minutes.

Flour two sheets of baking parchment and gently roll each ball into a 24-cm/9½-inch circle (or smaller if you prefer a thicker-crusted pizza). Slide each one carefully onto a baking sheet.

Add 150 g/¾ cup hummus on top of each rolled-out pizza base and use a spatula to distribute evenly. Top with onions, olives, garlic and mushrooms, and sprinkle ½ teaspoon of dried oregano/pizza seasoning over each pizza.

Open the heated oven, slide the baking paper with one pizza directly onto the bottom of the oven, without the baking sheet. Bake for 5 minutes. Change the oven setting to 'top grill/broiler', open the oven, slide the pizza with the baking parchment back onto the baking sheet and place the baking sheet in the upper part of the oven, so that the oven grill/broiler can quickly crisp the toppings. Bake for 2–3 minutes. Take out and repeat with the other pizza.

Just before serving, top pizzas with rocket/arugula, cherry tomatoes and a drizzle of olive oil.

rye open sandwiches

Denmark is a lovely travel destination and their *smørrebrød* open-sandwiches served as my inspiration here. Try to find Danish or German dense, dark-brown rye bread slices in your local food store to make these sandwiches, although any good-quality bread works well.

**4 teaspoons butter
or vegan butter**

**4 slices of dense sourdough
rye bread**

**300 g/1½ cup leftover
hummus (here we have used
Basic Hummus, page 12, Pea
and Basil Hummus, page 63,
and Beetroot/Beet Hummus,
page 24)**

**4 tablespoons sliced red
onion**

**4 crunchy pickles, roughly
chopped**

**8 cherry tomatoes (red
or green), cut in quarters**

1 bunch of dill, chopped

olive oil, for drizzling

MAKES 4 OPEN SANDWICHES

Spread butter over each slice of bread, add a generous amount of hummus, top with sliced onion, pickles, tomatoes and chopped dill. Drizzle with olive oil to serve.

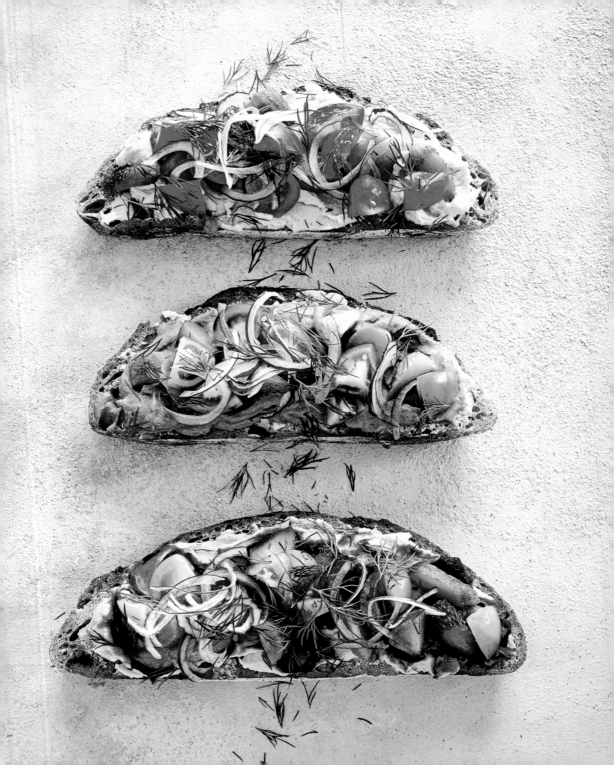

hummus salad dressings

Three of my favourite ways to give leftover hummus a chance to feel good about itself again, all dressed up as a salad dressing.

CAPER-INFUSED HUMMUS DRESSING

80 g/⅓ cup leftover hummus

2 teaspoons salt-cured capers

1 tablespoon olive oil

1 handful of fresh basil

1 tablespoon freshly squeezed lemon juice

60 ml/¼ cup water

SMOKY HUMMUS DRESSING

80 g/⅓ cup leftover hummus

3 tablespoons chopped onion

1 teaspoon smoked paprika

½ teaspoon sweet paprika

1 tablespoon sunflower oil

¼ teaspoon salt

1 tablespoon apple cider vinegar

60 ml/¼ cup water

freshly ground black pepper

GARLICKY HUMMUS DRESSING

80 g/⅓ cup leftover hummus

2–3 garlic cloves

¼ teaspoon salt

1 tablespoon olive oil

1 tablespoon freshly squeezed lemon juice, or to taste

½ teaspoon ground turmeric

60 ml/¼ cup soy or oat creamer

For each recipe, simply blend all the ingredients into a smooth dressing.

mushroom gravy

5 dried shiitake mushrooms or **7g/¼ cup dried porcini mushrooms**, soaked in 240 ml/1 cup warm water for 30 minutes, water reserved

90 g/3 oz. onions, sliced into thin half-moons

4 tablespoons light sesame oil

4 garlic cloves

1 tablespoon soy sauce

1 teaspoon apple cider vinegar

1 teaspoon rice/ agave syrup

100 g/½ cup leftover chickpea hummus

2 teaspoons Dijon mustard

2 tablespoons chopped greens (parsley, spring onions/scallions/ chives, etc.)

salt and freshly ground black pepper

MAKES ABOUT 480 ML/2 CUPS

Drain the soaked mushrooms, reserving the water. Discard the chewy stem (if using shiitake) and chop. In a big frying pan/skillet over low heat, sauté the onions in the oil with a pinch of salt until soft. Add the garlic and mushrooms and cook until fragrant. Raise the heat and add the soy sauce, vinegar and syrup. Stir until sizzling. Add the hummus and then slowly add the soaking water until a gravy consistency is reached. Add the mustard and some black pepper, taste and add more soy sauce if needed. Sprinkle with chopped greens, just before serving.

hummus pesto

50 g/1 handful of chard

240 ml/1 cup water

30 g/1 small bunch of fresh basil or parsley leaves

1 large garlic clove

3 tablespoons olive oil

¼ teaspoon salt

200 g/1 cup leftover chickpea-based hummus

hot water, if needed

TO SERVE

140 g/1¾ cups dry wholegrain penne pasta or 2 cups spiralized courgette/ zucchini, cooked

8 cherry tomatoes, cut in half

MAKES 300 G/ 1¼ CUPS, SERVES 2

Wash and remove the middle stems from the chard greens. Bring about 240 ml/1 cup of water to the boil and blanch the chard until soft but still bright green; about 2–3 minutes. Place the chard, basil or parsley, garlic, olive oil and salt into a small food processor or use a stick blender to blend all the ingredients into a chunky paste.

Stir the pesto paste into the hummus until well incorporated. Add a little hot water if too thick.

Serve on top of pasta or spiralized courgette/ zucchini, and add cherry tomatoes just before serving.

Sweet treats

cacao and rum hummus pudding with chickpea cream

Hummus dessert? Yup, it's true, and you will like it! Cooked chickpeas have a similar taste to cooked chestnuts, so I figured why not use chickpeas instead, and have this pudding all year round! Cacao powder, vanilla and cinnamon camouflage the mildly beany taste of chickpeas.

FOR THE CACAO HUMMUS

320 g/2 cups cooked chickpeas (see page 8-9), plus 60 ml/¼ cup of the cooking liquid, or more if needed

3–4 tablespoons dark agave syrup or maple syrup

3–4 tablespoons raw cacao powder

1 tablespoon rum (optional)

¼ teaspoon bourbon vanilla powder, or ½ teaspoon pure vanilla extract

¼ teaspoon Ceylon ground cinnamon

pinch of salt

FOR THE CREAM

120 ml/½ cup reserved chickpea cooking liquid, well chilled

¼ teaspoon bourbon vanilla powder

1 tablespoon maple sugar, or other

shaved dark/ bittersweet chocolate or cacao powder, to decorate

SERVES 2

For the cacao hummus, blend all of the ingredients into a creamy hummus, starting with 3 tablespoons of syrup and 3 tablespoons of cacao and adding enough cooking liquid to reach the desired consistency. Bear in mind that the pudding will thicken with time, so if you're not serving it right away, make it a touch softer. Taste and see if you want to add more cacao or syrup, or both.

For the whipped cream, whisk the chilled chickpea liquid with a hand mixer until soft peaks are formed. Add the vanilla and sugar and whisk to form semi-firm peaks. Use immediately or whisk again briefly before using (some liquid might separate, if not used straight away).

Serve the whipped cream on top of the pudding and decorate with shaves of dark/bittersweet chocolate or sift some cacao powder on top. No one will be able to tell that the main ingredient for this dessert is chickpeas.

carob hummus mousse

FOR THE MOUSSE

320 g/2 cups cooked chickpeas (see page 8–9), plus 240 ml/1 cup of the cooking liquid

20 g/2 tablespoons cacao butter

2 tablespoons fine carob powder (or swap for cacao powder or grain coffee if you like)

3 tablespoons maple or agave syrup

¼ teaspoon bourbon vanilla sugar

2 tablespoons fresh raspberries, to serve

FOR THE GARNISH

2 teaspoons maple syrup

1 teaspoon maple sugar (used to bind ingredients)

½ teaspoon Ceylon cinnamon

¼ teaspoon allspice

¼ teaspoon bourbon vanilla sugar

baking sheet lined with baking parchment

SERVES 2

Instead of cacao, why not use another superfood once in a while – the aromatic carob, for example. It's sweet, nutritious and pairs well with cacao butter and whipped chickpea cream!

For the mousse, first whip the chickpea cooking liquid with a stand mixer in a bigger bowl, for about 4 minutes or until soft peaks start forming. If done correctly, it should triple in size.

In a double boiler, melt the cacao butter. Set aside half of the chickpeas for the garnish. Place the other half of the chickpeas, melted cacao butter, carob powder, syrup, vanilla sugar and whipped chickpea cream in a blender and start blending, using a tamper to push down the ingredients. Blend for 1 minute, or until velvety. Cover and refrigerate for at least 3 hours.

For the garnish, preheat the oven to 220°C (425°F) Gas 7.

Place just the reserved chickpeas for the garnish on the lined baking sheet. Bake in the preheated oven for 25 minutes or until golden and slightly crunchy. Immediately after baking, place them into a bowl and add the remaining ingredients. Mix thoroughly. Use warm as a garnish for this dessert, or store for later (although they are best when freshly made). If using later, put back into the hot oven for about 5 minutes.

Divide the chilled mousse into two dessert glasses, add the raspberries and top with 2 tablespoons garnish per portion. Serve immediately.

fudge cookies

This is another tasty bean-based treat that even children will enjoy, without knowing they're having chickpeas. These fudge cookies will satisfy your chocolate craving the minute you bite into one!

60 g/½ cup 70% dark/ bittersweet vegan chocolate

160 g/1 cup cooked chickpeas

65 g/⅓ cup sunflower or coconut oil

200 g/¾ cup rice, maple or agave syrup

½ teaspoon apple cider vinegar

130 g/1 cup plain/all-purpose flour

2 tablespoons cacao powder

½ teaspoon baking powder

½ teaspoon bicarbonate of soda/baking soda

¼ teaspoon salt

soy milk, as needed

baking sheet lined with baking parchment

MAKES ABOUT 24 COOKIES

In a double-boiler, melt the chocolate and keep it over the hot water so it stays runny.

Blend the chickpeas, oil, syrup and vinegar in a food processor or blender. Add the melted chocolate and transfer to a bowl.

Preheat the oven to 180°C (360°F) Gas 4.

Take a big sieve/strainer and place it on top of the bowl with the liquid ingredients (this way you won't have to use two separate bowls). Sift the flour, cacao powder, baking powder, bicarbonate of soda/baking soda and salt through the sieve/strainer, using a whisk to help it through. Use a spatula to incorporate all the ingredients into a smooth batter, adding soy milk to reach the necessary consistency – it should not slide down the spoon. If it does, chill the batter in the fridge for 10 minutes before continuing.

Drop the batter onto the lined baking sheet using a tablespoon, placing the drops 1 cm/⅜ inch apart. Bake in the preheated oven for 12–14 minutes. The dough is dark to start with so it's easy to burn the cookies. You want them still soft to the touch when they are out of the oven, so check for doneness after 12 minutes, and bake them no longer than 14 minutes! The baking time is essential; 1 minute too long and they will not stay soft and gooey.

Slide the baking parchment with the cookies onto the kitchen counter or onto a cold tray and let cool. Store in a cookie jar for a week or so.

hummus and walnut crêpes

When I was young, one of the special winter treats at my grandma's house were her walnut-filled pancakes. This is my dairy-free and sugar-free version, which tastes every bit as good as I remember from my childhood – and they are much healthier, too!

FOR THE CRÊPES

165 ml/¾ cup soy milk

110 ml/½ cup sparkling water

¼ teaspoon salt

¼ teaspoon baking powder

130 g/1 cup plain/all-purpose or spelt flour

coconut oil, for frying

FOR THE FILLING

140 g/1 cup walnuts

160 g/1 cup cooked chickpeas (see page 8–9)

160 g/16 stoned/pitted dates

½ teaspoon pure vanilla extract

240 ml/1 cup plant-based milk, warmed

sliced strawberries, maple syrup and vegan vanilla ice cream, to serve

SERVES 4

For the crêpes, combine the soy milk and water. Do not substitute soy milk with other plant-based milks or the crêpes will fall apart. Add the salt and baking powder. Slowly add the flour, whisking vigorously. The batter should be thicker than a usual egg pancake batter. Let sit for 15 minutes, or longer.

Heat a cast-iron frying pan/skillet and brush with coconut oil before each new crêpe. Pour a small ladleful of batter into the pan and spread evenly, approximately 20 cm/8 inches in diameter. Once the edges turn golden brown, turn over and fry for another minute.

For the filling, preheat the oven to 180°C (360°F) Gas 4.

Spread the walnuts onto a baking sheet and dry-roast until golden (be careful, walnuts burn easily); about 8–10 minutes. Stir once during baking. Grind the roasted walnuts into a fine flour. This step can be done well in advance. Set aside 2 tablespoons to serve.

Blend the chickpeas with the dates, vanilla and milk until smooth; about 1 minute. Stir in the ground walnuts.

Place 1 full tablespoon (about 60 g/2¼ oz.) of filling on the bottom half of each pancake, spread evenly and fold with the upper half. Fold once again to get a triangle. Some of the filling should spill out a little – this makes them very appetizing.

Drizzle with maple syrup and sprinkle the reserved ground walnuts on top, just before serving. Decorate with sliced strawberries or other berries and serve with vegan vanilla ice cream, if you like.

hummus brownies

At first, the idea of using hummus in a brownie dough doesn't sound too promising. However, it gives a wonderful texture to the brownie and it's a great way to introduce plant protein to kids – or even grown ups!

200 g/1½ cups 70% dark/bittersweet vegan chocolate

400 g/2 cups Cacao Hummus (see page 116)

65 g/⅓ cup sunflower oil

130 g/½ cup brown rice, agave or maple syrup

grated zest and freshly squeezed juice of 1 lemon

85 g/⅔ cup plain/all-purpose flour

40 g/⅓ cup wholemeal/whole-wheat flour

8 g/2 teaspoons aluminium-free baking powder

9 g/1 ½ teaspoons baking/bicarbonate of soda

2 g/scant ½ teaspoon salt

1 g/¼ teaspoon ground cinnamon

80 g/½ cup whole walnuts, or 80 g/1 cup finely ground walnuts

2 tablespoons apricot jam, to serve

23 x 30-cm/9 x 12-inch baking pan, well oiled

MAKES 12 BROWNIES

Preheat the oven to 180°C (360°F) Gas 4.

Melt the chocolate in a double-boiler. In a food processor, or using a stick blender, blend the melted chocolate, cacao hummus, oil, syrup, lemon zest and juice until smooth.

Take a big sieve/strainer and place it on top of the bowl with the liquid ingredients (this way you won't have to use two separate bowls). Sift the flours, baking powder, bicarbonate of soda/baking soda salt and cinnamon through the sieve/strainer, using a whisk to help it through. Add the walnuts.

Combine the dry ingredients with the chocolate mix, folding with a spatula until you get a smooth, thick batter (much thicker than usual cake batters).

Spoon the batter into the baking pan and use a spatula to even the surface; if it sticks too much, wet the spatula under warm water.

Bake in the preheated oven for 20–25 minutes. Do not over-bake; they are supposed to be a little gooey! I like to serve them with little home-made apricot jam

ice-cream cups

Chickpeas have been used for desserts since Roman times, it's not a new thing. I encourage you to try this delicious ice-cream!

3 ripe bananas

100 g/½ cup leftover Cacao Hummus (see page 116)

¼ teaspoon Bourbon vanilla powder or 1 teaspoon pure vanilla extract

2 tablespoons cacao nibs, plus extra to decorate

1 teaspoon coconut oil

60 ml/¼ cup coconut milk, if necessary (for weaker blenders)

2 tablespoons maple or agave syrup, to serve

shaved coconut flakes and fresh cherries, to decorate

SERVES 2

Peel and chop the bananas. Freeze the banana pieces on a small tray placed directly in the freezer. You can do this a day ahead. Before blending, let the bananas sit at room temperature for a couple of minutes. Blend all the ingredients in a high-speed blender for 1–2 minutes, pushing down the ingredients with the tamper tool. Start with low speed and increase slowly. (Note: If you own a weaker blender, let the frozen banana sit at room temperature for 10 minutes until they are easier to blend. However, the texture of the ice-cream won't be as creamy.)

Serve immediately in ice-cream cups, drizzled with syrup, sprinkled with coconut flakes and cacao nibs and garnished with fresh cherries.

Index

acknowledgements

As with all my cookbooks, I'd like to thank my family, friends and especially the people who follow my work for their support, enthusiasm and trust. I get emails and messages from people all over the world on a weekly basis, letting me know that they are using my recipes and how much some things I have written and shared have changed their diets for the better. I get photos of my dishes made by others all the time too – it's such a good feeling knowing my books aren't just a decoration on kitchen shelves. Instead, they are actually being used. That is what keeps me motivated to continue with what I'm doing!

I'd also like to thank the whole RPS team, above all Julia Charles for her support over the years, Sonya Nathoo for her gorgeous design work and Alice Sambrook for her patience and flexibility with deadlines! Thank you also to Mowie Kay, Emily Kydd and Jo Harris for the beautiful photography, I'm so grateful to be surrounded by a creative and supportive team.

Finally, I'd like to thank you for choosing this book as your cooking companion! It will bring tasty and nourishing dishes to your family table, and I hope that you will feel the pinch of passion secretly added to each and every one of the recipes in this cookbook – that tiny ingredient can make a gigantic difference!